Travis Kelce

Charlie Beattie

childsworld.com

The Child's World®
childsworld.com

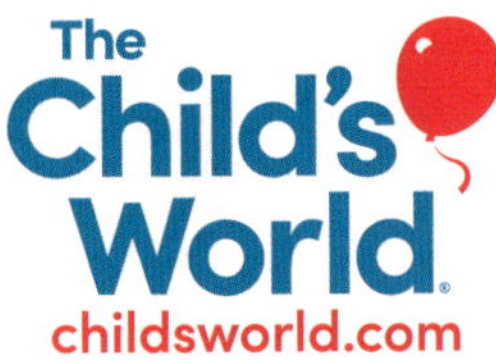

Published by The Child's World®
800-599-READ • www.childsworld.com

Photography Credits
Photographs ©: Joe Mahoney/AP Images, cover, 1; Kit Leong/Shutterstock Images, 5; Ringo Chiu/Shutterstock Images, 6; Debby Wong/Shutterstock Images, 7; Erik Dost/Flickr, 9; Shutterstock Images, 10, 23, 25; Jim Owens/Icon Sportswire, 13; Jeremy McKnight/Icon Sportswire, 14; Justin Edmonds/Getty Images Sport/Getty Images, 17; Jamie Lamor Thompson/Shutterstock Images, 19; Kyle Rivas/Getty Images Entertainment/Getty Images, 20; Michael Owens/Getty Images Sport/Getty Images, 27; Hannah Foslien/White House, 28; Design elements from Shutterstock Images

ISBN Information
9781503875739 (Reinforced Library Binding)
9781503876729 (Portable Document Format)
9781503877221 (Online Multi-user eBook)
9781503877849 (Electronic Publication)

LCCN 2025938205

Printed in the United States of America

BRINGING THE WORLD TO YOUNG READERS 1968

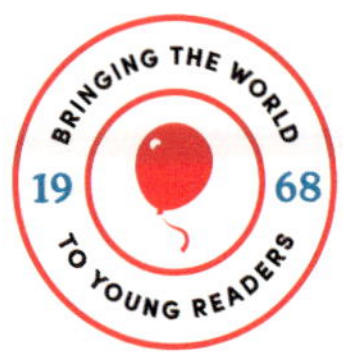

ABOUT THE AUTHOR

Charlie Beattie is an editor, writer, and former sportscaster. Originally from Saint Paul, Minnesota, he now lives in Charleston, South Carolina, with his wife and son.

TABLE of CONTENTS

CHAPTER ONE

Clutch Catch

It was February 11, 2024, and the Kansas City Chiefs needed a big play. They trailed the San Francisco 49ers 19–16 with 16 seconds left in Super Bowl LVII. Kansas City was at the San Francisco 33-yard line. It was third down with 7 yards to go.

Chiefs tight end Travis Kelce lined up at the right end of the offensive line. Quarterback Patrick Mahomes took the snap. Kelce took a quick step forward. He faked to his right. Then he bolted to the left. San Francisco linebacker Fred Warner could not keep up. Kelce was sprinting across the field when he caught Mahomes's pass. Kelce then turned toward the end zone.

RECORD SETTER

The Kansas City Chiefs beat the Baltimore Ravens 17–10 to reach Super Bowl LVIII. During the game, Kelce caught his 152nd career postseason pass. That broke a tie with legendary wide receiver Jerry Rice for the most catches by any player in the playoffs.

Super Bowl LVIII was played at Allegiant Stadium in Las Vegas, Nevada. About 123.4 million viewers watched the game.

The team colors of the Kansas City Chiefs are red and gold.

Several defenders tried to cut him off. But Kelce had enough speed to get to the sideline. He sprinted 22 yards before a 49ers defensive back knocked the big tight end out of bounds at the 8-yard line. Two plays later, the Chiefs tied the game on a field goal. The Chiefs eventually won 25–22 in **overtime**.

Travis Kelce is used to making big plays. In his National Football League (NFL) career, he became one of the greatest tight ends. He also rose to fame as a huge celebrity in the entertainment world. He is a successful podcaster, actor, and television personality. In 2023, he began dating Taylor Swift, one of the most famous musicians on the planet. Both on and off the field, Kelce is used to the spotlight.

In 2023, Kelce attended the Country Music Television (CMT) Music Awards.

CHAPTER TWO

Growing Up Kelce

Travis Kelce was born in Westlake, Ohio, on October 5, 1989. He grew up in a family that was **enthusiastic** about sports. His father, Ed, played football. Travis's mother, Donna, competed in track and field. Travis and his older brother Jason played several sports. Travis was an excellent baseball and basketball player. But he was at his best on the football field.

Travis played quarterback for Cleveland Heights High School. But not many colleges were interested in offering him a **scholarship**. Travis eventually signed to play at the University of Cincinnati. The school had offered him a scholarship. He joined Jason, who was already playing for the Bearcats as an offensive lineman.

Travis loved playing all kinds of sports growing up. In 2021, he played in a celebrity softball game.

The University of Cincinnati is in Ohio. It is about a 4-hour drive from Travis's hometown.

Travis took a redshirt year during his first college season in 2008. This meant he practiced with the team, but he was not allowed to play in games. The next year, he did not get on the field much. He ran for two touchdowns as a quarterback. The Bearcats coaches also used him as a tight end. But Travis caught only one pass.

Travis made a huge mistake before the 2010 season. He was caught with illegal drugs. The Cincinnati coaches **suspended** him. They were thinking of kicking him off the team. But Jason was one of the Bearcats' captains. He convinced the coaches to give his younger brother another chance. Travis was eventually invited back to the team. But he had to sit out during the season. If Travis got in trouble again, he would be gone for good.

Travis played tight end full-time when he came back to the team. He was not a star player. By the end of the 2011 season, Travis had caught only 13 passes for Cincinnati. But he stayed out of trouble. He focused on football and his education. He had one more year to prove he could play professional football.

By the time the 2012 season started, Travis was tough to defend at the tight end position. At 6 feet 5 inches (1.96 m), he was too tall for most defensive backs. But he was too fast and athletic for linebackers. Travis had more than 700 receiving yards. He was also a team leader. He often gave speeches to his teammates before games to fire them up.

Travis pumped up the crowd during a game against the Rutgers Scarlet Knights in 2012.

Travis celebrated with fans after the Belk Bowl win against Duke.

Travis saved his best play for his last game. Cincinnati played Duke in the Belk Bowl at the end of the year. The teams were tied 34–34 with under a minute left. Cincinnati had the ball at its own 17-yard line. Travis sprinted down the middle of the field. The Bearcats' quarterback fired a pass that Travis caught at full speed. He pulled away from the Blue Devils' defenders for a game-winning 83-yard touchdown catch!

By that game, NFL coaches knew about Travis's skills. One coach who liked him was Andy Reid of the Kansas City Chiefs. But he was worried about the trouble Travis had gotten into. Reid had coached Jason with the Philadelphia Eagles. Reid asked Jason if he could trust Travis to be a professional player. Once again, Jason stuck up for his younger brother. The Chiefs took Travis in the third round of the 2013 **draft**. He was off to start his NFL career.

FINISHING SCHOOL

Travis left school for the NFL before he could finish his degree. But in 2022, he finished his last credits to get a degree in interdisciplinary studies. Interdisciplinary studies combines more than one educational field for students who want to create a new topic. Travis received his diploma in 2024. He and Jason were recording a podcast episode inside Cincinnati's basketball arena. Travis received his diploma during the show.

CHAPTER THREE

A Superstar

Travis Kelce's professional career got off to a slow start. He injured his knee during the preseason. Kelce tried to play anyway. But he only got on the field for one play in the season's second game. Afterward, team doctors examined his knee again. They said he needed knee surgery. He would miss the rest of the season. But he knew it would help his knee feel better.

As soon as Kelce's knee was healed, he quickly became a top player. Kelce caught 67 passes during the 2014 season. The next year, he caught 72. After the season, he was named to the Pro Bowl for the first time. The Pro Bowl happens a week before the Super Bowl. It hosts games between some of the best NFL players. Kelce also signed a big new contract. Before the 2016 season, the Chiefs agreed to pay Kelce $46 million over the next 5 years.

Football is a contact sport. Players often collide with other players and risk injury.

Kelce also got his first starring role off the field. During the summer of 2016, he filmed a reality show called *Catching Kelce*. The dating show featured one contestant from each US state. The contestants tried to win Kelce's heart. Each week, he gave contestants footballs if they passed to the next round. Kelce said making the show was fun. But he did not think it was very good.

Things were better on the field. Kelce was one of the NFL's best tight ends. In 2016, he made the All-Pro team for the first time. It recognizes the best players at each position. And the Chiefs were also a winning team. They made the playoffs every year starting in 2015. In January 2018, Kelce caught his first playoff touchdown against the Tennessee Titans. But the Chiefs lost the game 22–21.

Kelce attended the Shaq's Fun House event in 2019. It had live music and performances.

Kelce and Mahomes have developed a close friendship on and off the field. In 2024, they attended a charity event called Big Slick.

Patrick Mahomes became Kansas City's starting quarterback in 2019. He quickly became a superstar. Mahomes and Kelce nearly led the Chiefs to the Super Bowl that season. The following year, the Chiefs went 12–4. Many football fans expected them to win it all. But things were looking bad in their first playoff game. The Chiefs fell behind the Houston Texans in the second quarter.

Kelce and Mahomes stepped up. Mahomes threw four touchdown passes before halftime. Kelce caught three of them. Kansas City went on to win 51–31. The Chiefs then beat the Titans 35–24. That win put them in Super Bowl LIV against the San Francisco 49ers.

BROTHERLY LOVE

In 2011, Jason Kelce was drafted by the Philadelphia Eagles. He quickly became one of the best centers in the NFL. Jason helped the Eagles win their first Super Bowl title in February 2018. Five years later, the Eagles and Chiefs played each other in Super Bowl LVII. Jason and Travis became the first brothers to ever play each other in the Super Bowl.

The Chiefs had not won a Super Bowl for 50 years. Their fans were worried that streak would continue when Kansas City was down 20–10 with 9 minutes left. But Mahomes guided Kansas City to the San Francisco 1-yard line with just over 6 minutes to go. Kelce broke off the line and cut to the right side of the field. He was wide open. Mahomes tossed him an easy touchdown pass.

The score started a Kansas City rally. The Chiefs won the game 31–20. Kelce was a Super Bowl champion. And he and his teammates were just getting started.

TRAVIS KELCE'S NFL CAREER BY THE NUMBERS

In the NFL, Travis Kelce has gained success and fame. These are Kelce's NFL achievements as of the end of the 2024 season.

DRAFTED

Third round, pick 63,
2013 NFL Draft
(Kansas City Chiefs)

REGULAR SEASON RECEIVING TOTALS

1,004 receptions, 12,151 yards,
77 touchdowns

10 PRO BOWL APPEARANCES

FOUR-TIME FIRST-TEAM ALL-PRO

THREE-TIME SUPER BOWL CHAMPION

A RECORD 35 RECEPTIONS IN SUPER BOWLS

CHAPTER FOUR

World Famous

In the early 2020s, the Chiefs were one of the NFL's top teams. Kelce was a big reason why. The standout tight end was nearly unstoppable on the field. In 2022, he caught a career-high 110 passes. He hauled in 27 more in the playoffs, including four touchdowns. The Chiefs won the Super Bowl again in 2023. They beat the Philadelphia Eagles 38–35.

Kelce was also becoming a bigger star off the field. He launched a successful podcast with his brother in 2022. Three weeks after winning the Super Bowl, he hosted *Saturday Night Live*. It was the first time many fans had seen him off the field. The sketch comedy show put his sense of humor and **charisma** on display. Reviewers thought the episode was a huge hit.

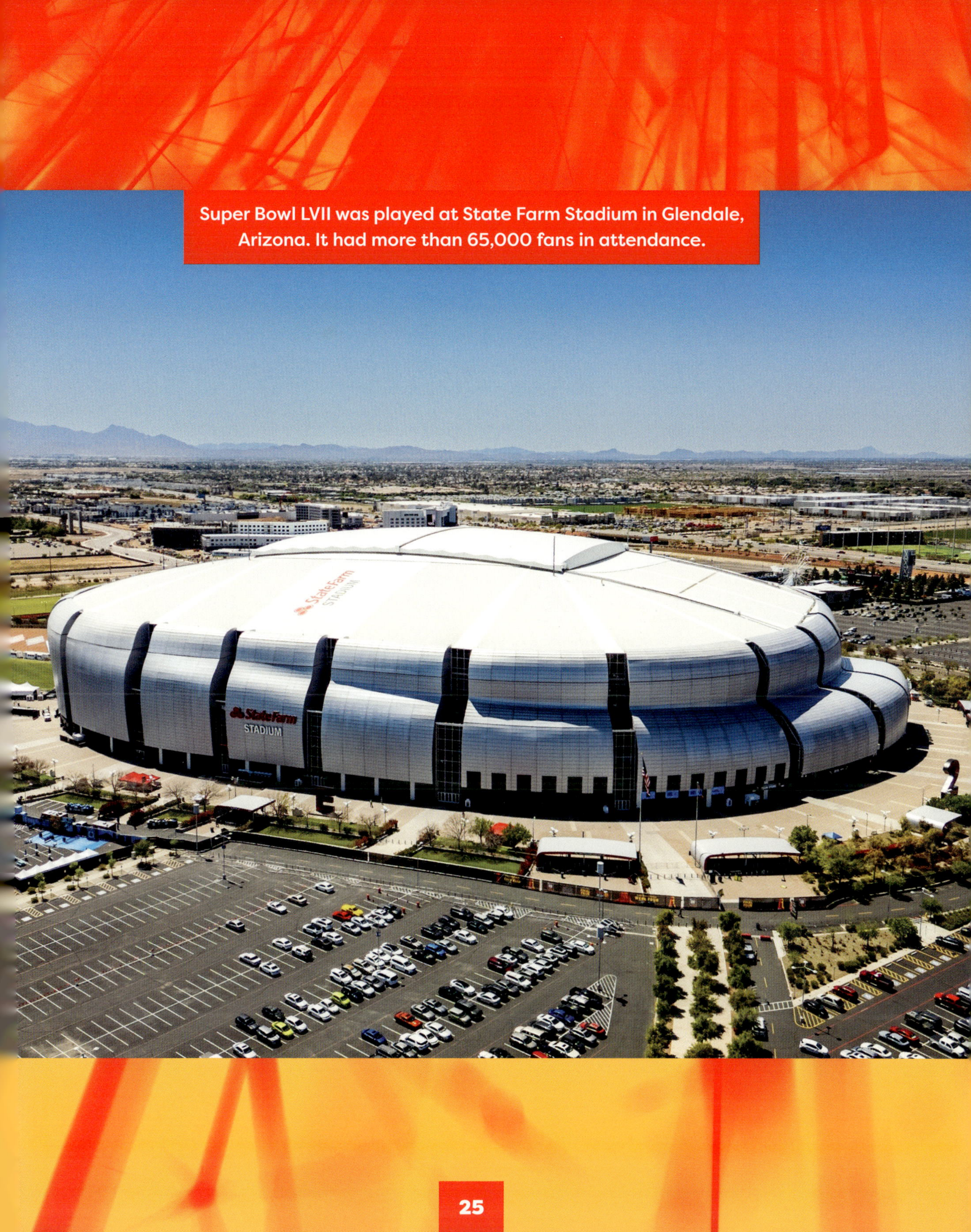

Super Bowl LVII was played at State Farm Stadium in Glendale, Arizona. It had more than 65,000 fans in attendance.

Kelce was enjoying his time in the entertainment world. That April, he hosted a concert festival outside Kansas City called "Kelce Jam." Kelce entertained the crowd between musical acts. He called it one of the most fun things he had ever done.

Later that summer, rumors swirled that Kelce was dating pop star Taylor Swift. The couple confirmed their relationship in September 2023. That fall, the singer came to many of Kansas City's games. She was in the middle of a worldwide concert tour. But Swift often flew in from cities around the globe to support Kelce.

TAKING THE STAGE

Just as Swift had supported Kelce on the field, he made sure to get to her shows. At one show in London in June 2024, Kelce surprised audiences. He wore a full tuxedo, complete with a top hat. Kelce helped Swift perform a scripted introduction to her song "I Can Do It With a Broken Heart."

Swift supported Kelce at his games. She brought many new fans to the Kansas City Chiefs.

Swift's craziest journey came before Super Bowl LVIII. Swift was performing in Japan the night before the game. But after her show, she hopped on a plane. She made it to Las Vegas just before the Chiefs kicked off against the San Francisco 49ers. Swift cheered wildly as Kelce helped Kansas City tie the game late to force overtime. In overtime, the Chiefs moved the ball to the San Francisco 1-yard line. They were down 22–19.

Travis Kelce and the Chiefs met with President Joe Biden in May 2024 to celebrate their Super Bowl LVIII win.

Kansas City could win the game. Coach Andy Reid knew the 49ers would be watching Kelce closely. The coach decided to use Kelce as a **decoy**. Kelce lined up wide to the right. Receiver Mecole Hardman was next to Kelce. At the snap, Kelce ran in front of Hardman and toward the middle of the field. Hardman ran toward the sideline. Hardman's defender tried to get to him. But he ran into Kelce instead. Hardman was wide open for the game-winning touchdown. After the game, Swift and Kelce celebrated the star tight end's third Super Bowl win on the field.

Kelce and the Chiefs were looking to make NFL history in 2025. No team had ever won three Super Bowls in a row. Kansas City reached the big game again and faced the Eagles. This time, Philadelphia came out on top 40–22. But late in the game, Kelce caught his 34th career Super Bowl pass. That was a new NFL record.

Chiefs fans were worried that Kelce was going to retire after the season. He said he needed time to think about it. He was busy balancing his podcast and work in both film and acting. But Kelce still loved football. A few weeks after the game, he said he was coming back for at least one more season. He wanted to go out on top.

IN HIS WORDS

In 2015, Kelce created the "87 and Running" foundation, which provides educational programs for underserved communities in Kansas City. He said:

"I wanted to make sure the people here in Kansas City felt my support the way I feel their support on game days."

Source: "Travis Kelce on How His Foundation Has Helped Underserved Communities in KC, Cleveland." NFL Game Day Morning, *n.d. www.nfl.com/videos.*

GLOSSARY

charisma (kuh-RIZ-muh) Charisma is a person's natural charm that often draws or attracts others. Kelce's charisma came through in his podcast and other off-field projects.

decoy (DEE-koy) A decoy is something that is used to distract someone. Kelce was used as a decoy to help the Chiefs score the winning touchdown of Super Bowl LVIII.

diploma (dih-PLOH-muh) A diploma is a certificate given to a student to show that they have completed their studies. Kelce earned his college diploma in 2024.

draft (DRAFT) A draft is the process of teams picking new players, usually out of college. The Chiefs took Kelce in the third round of the 2013 draft.

enthusiastic (en-thoo-zee-AS-tik) An enthusiastic person is showing excitement or joy. Kelce was an enthusiastic person on his football team.

legendary (LEH-jun-deh-ree) Something legendary is well-known. Kelce is a legendary tight end.

overtime (OH-ver-tym) Overtime is an extra period of play at the end of a tied sports contest to decide a winner. In the NFL, overtime is a 10-minute period added on to the end of a tied game.

scholarship (SKA-lur-ship) A scholarship is money given to someone to help pay for their education. Kelce received a scholarship to go to the University of Cincinnati.

suspended (suh-SPEN-did) When someone is suspended, they are removed from an activity for a period of time as a punishment. Kelce was suspended from the Bearcats after doing illegal drugs.

FAST FACTS

- ★ Travis Kelce was born on October 5, 1989. He grew up in Cleveland Heights, Ohio, with his parents, Ed and Donna, and his older brother, Jason.
- ★ Kelce attended the University of Cincinnati, where he played tight end and quarterback. Kelce was eventually drafted by the Kansas City Chiefs in the third round of the 2013 NFL Draft.
- ★ Kelce won his first Super Bowl in February 2019. He caught a touchdown pass in the fourth quarter of the 31–20 victory over the San Francisco 49ers.
- ★ Travis and Jason Kelce were the first brothers to compete against one another in the Super Bowl in February 2023. Travis's Chiefs beat Jason's Philadelphia Eagles 38–35.
- ★ Kelce and pop star Taylor Swift began dating in 2023. Swift watched Kelce win the Super Bowl in February 2024.

ONE STRIDE FURTHER

- ★ Kelce has had many great accomplishments. What are some of your greatest achievements? Did you do them alone, or did you have a team to help you?
- ★ Kelce worked hard to be a successful football player. What are some challenges you have faced while working toward a goal? How did you overcome them?
- ★ Jason helped Travis throughout his football career. Are there times people have helped you achieve your goals? How did that make you feel? Why is supporting others important?

FIND OUT MORE

IN THE LIBRARY

Anderson, Josh. *Inside the Kansas City Chiefs.* Minneapolis, MN: Lerner, 2024.

Rose, Lisa. *Taylor Swift.* Parker, CO: The Child's World, 2026.

Shulman, Mark, and Solomon Shulman. *Football Superstars.* Parker, CO: The Child's World, 2023.

ON THE WEB

Visit our website for links about Travis Kelce:

childsworld.com/links

Note to Parents, Caregivers, Teachers, and Librarians: We routinely verify our web links to make sure they are safe and active sites. So encourage your readers to check them out!

INDEX